FRESH GROSS JOKES

A man walked into a newspaper office and told the girl in the classified department, "I want to put an ad in the paper. My wife's cat is missing and I'm offering a $10,000 reward."

The girl was shocked. "Isn't that an enormous amount of money for a cat?"

The guy grinned. "No, it isn't. I drowned the cat yesterday."

Why does Dan Quayle enjoy having a cold?

It's the only thing he can keep in his head for more than a minute.

A cannibal wife stormed up to her husband and demanded, "Who was that lady I saw you with last night?"

The husband replied, "That was no lady, that was my dinner."

Fresh GROSS JOKES

Volume VII

By Julius Alvin

ZEBRA BOOKS
KENSINGTON PUBLISHING CORP.

ZEBRA BOOKS

are published by

Kensington Publishing Corp.
475 Park Avenue South
New York, NY 10016

First printing: April, 1989

Printed in the United States of America

For Bill and Val, this joke series' biggest fans, who've probably bought more GROSS JOKES *books than the rest of the world combined*

TABLE OF CONTENTS

Chapter One

Gross Ethnic and Racial Jokes

How does a WASP housewife know dinner is ready?

The smoke alarm goes off.

The wealthy couple hired a Polish caretaker to do some work around their estate while they toured Europe. A month later, they arrived home during a violent rainstorm. To their great horror, they walked into their living room to find the Polack sitting in the middle of the floor while water poured from the ceiling.

"You idiot!" the man shouted. "I told you about that roof. Get up there right now and stop that leak."

"Can't," the Polack replied. "It's raining too hard."

"Well, why didn't you fix it when it wasn't raining outside."

"Because," the Polack replied, "it wasn't leaking then."

Why are the sturdiest chairs always made out of kosher wood?

They never tip.

One Russian came up to another and said, "Did you hear the awful news? The coach of our Olympic hockey team died after they lost the gold medal match to the Americans."

"No!" the other one exclaimed. "When did he die?"

The first Russian replied, "Tomorrow."

The young producer came to the studio with the script for a film that would tell the complete story of a huge slave rebellion in the pre-Civil War South. The head of the studio told him, "Hal, baby, this is a dynamite script, best I've read in years. But there's no way it can be made. Why, you have one scene alone, the one where the white soldiers fire on five thousand slaves, would cost 10 million bucks. The whole picture would cost us $100 million."

The young producer acknowledged the problem, but begged for some time to come up with a solution. He came back a week later and said, "J.B., I've contacted the Mississippi prison system. They'll let us use prisoners as extras for $10 a piece a day. That will save us millions."

The head of the studio called in his head accountant, and they did some figuring. Finally, he said to the producer, "Sorry, Hal. Using prisoners at 10 dollars a day will save you 30 million. But the film's still too expensive. We won't spend a dime over 30 million to make the film."

The producer thought for a moment, then said, "What if I shoot in Africa? Over there, extras work for 3 or 4 dollars a day."

The accountant did some more figuring, then shook his head. "For the number of days you need to shoot, even that's too much."

The producer thought again, then said, "J.B., I've got a proposal. If I can make this picture for 30 million dollars, will you buy it?"

The studio head said, "Sure. But it's got to be the same picture—no cutting back on all those battle scenes."

The producer agreed. No one heard from him for almost two months. One day, he showed up with the entire movie under his arm. The head of the studio was skeptical, but he became enthusiastic as he viewed the product. "I don't see how you did it, Hal.

Those battle scenes—I don't know how you could afford so many extras. And they were so convincing besides. Tell me, what's the secret?"

The producer grinned. "Easy. I convinced the South African Army to let me use their white soldiers for nothing because it was a training exercise. Of course," he added, "I did have to let them use real bullets."

The Polack had just been introduced to his date, and they started to dance. Suddenly the Polack thrust his hand into her pants and shoved a finger up her ass.

Startled and angry, the woman jumped back and yelled, "Gross."

So the Polack did it 143 more times.

Why did the Polish housewife serve curry with baked beans?

She loved Indian music.

What's the first thing a WASP learns about gardening?

To turn the soil over—to a gardener.

How can you tell if a limousine is owned by a Jew?

There's a pay phone in the backseat.

Did you hear about the Polack who stayed up all night trying to figure out where the sun went when it set?

Then it finally dawned on him.

Did you hear about the guy who ran into a Puerto Rican bar and yelled, "Fire!"?

Everyone did.

One Polack came up to another and said, "Come on over to my house for dinner. I've got three big rabbits to roast."

The second Polack said, "Rabbits are very expensive. How did you manage to afford three?"

The first Polack said, "Oh, I can get all the rabbits I want. Every night they're out in the alley behind my house going, 'Meow, meow, meow.'"

The Polack's girlfriend always wanted to fly, so for her birthday he chartered a small plane for a ride over New York City. The two strapped themselves in behind the pilot and the plane took off. As they cruised over the nation's largest city, the Polack tried to show off. He pointed to a building and said, "Hey, that's the Empire State Building."

The pilot, hearing him, leaned back and said, "Wrong, pal. That's the Chrysler Building."

The Polack grimaced. A moment later he pointed and said to his girl, "Hey, that's Shea Stadium."

The pilot once again leaned back and said, "Wrong, pal. That's Yankee Stadium."

The Polack's face turned red. But before he had a chance to do anything, the engine on the plane started to sputter, then conked out. Hurriedly, the pilot strapped a parachute on, then handed parachutes to the Polack and his girlfriend. After they put them on, he said, "Put these on. Then jump clear of the plane, count to ten, and pull this ripcord." Then the pilot jumped.

The Polack and his girlfriend jumped side by side. As they cleared the plane, the girl noticed the Polack was laughing hysterically. She shouted, "What's so funny?"

The Polack replied, "That pilot thinks he knows everything. But he didn't know I can't count to ten."

Why did the Polish burglar break two windows?

One to get in, and one to get out.

Did you hear about the Eskimo woman who spent the night with her boyfriend?

When she woke up, she was six months pregnant.

Why don't Russian women wear yellow?

So people don't yell "Taxi!" at them.

Why do Polish men wear cuffs on their pants?

To catch their dandruff.

How do you get a Mississippi black out of a tree?

Cut the rope.

Did you hear about the new laid-back California church?

It has four commandments and six suggestions.

One guy came up to his buddy and said, "I've got to talk to you about that Chinese girl you set me up with. You told me she was a Poster Girl of the Year."

The friend said, "So?"

The first guy said, "You didn't tell me it was the Year of the Dog."

Why do Arab women wear veils over their faces?

So they can blow their noses without using their hands.

Why did the Polack water half his lawn?

Because the weatherman said there was a 50 percent chance of rain.

How can you tell a drunk is Polish?

He's the one French-kissing the fire hydrant outside the bar.

What's a Jewish "10?"

A girl with 4 limbs and 6 million dollars.

Did you hear about the Jewish Santa Claus?

He comes down the chimney, wakes the kids, then says, "Hey, you wanna buy some toys cheap?"

Did you hear about the Polish coyote?

He chewed off three legs and he was still caught in the trap.

What do they call diarrhea in Harlem?

Brain drain.

What's round, is red and white, and is covered with flies?

A Polish pizza.

What's it called when you play a game of wits with a Polack?

Solitaire.

How can you recognize the Polish motorcycle gang?

Their motorcycles have air conditioners.

What's the Puerto Rican national flower?

Mildew.

How many people does it take to bury a Polack?

Eight. Six to carry the casket and two to drag the body.

Why did the Polack buy a farm in Alaska?

He wanted to grow frozen vegetables.

What's the difference between a JAP and a toilet seat?

A toilet seat warms up when you touch it.

Why don't flies buzz Italians?

Even flies have some pride.

How can you tell a man is a WASP?

His favorite food is cheese and crackers.

Stanislaus rushed into the house one day and shouted to his Polish father, "Papa, I got an A in spelling."

His father slapped him so hard he flew across the room. "You idiot," the father shouted, "there ain't no A in spelling."

The priest heard that the new Polish family in the parish was blessed with a new arrival. He stopped by the house and said to the father, "I'd like to schedule the christening as soon as possible."

"No way!" the Polack exclaimed. "We had three other babies die doing that?"

The puzzled priest asked, "How could a baby die from being bathed in holy water?"

"It weren't the water," the Polack replied. "It was hitting them over the head with the bottle."

The boss called the Italian into his office and said, "Son, you're a hard worker. I want to send you to a course that tells you how to get ahead."

"I don't wanna go," the Italian replied.

"Why?" the boss asked.

"I already got a head."

A Polish housewife came home one day to find her husband furiously masturbating in the middle of the kitchen. "What are you doing?" she cried.

"I'm baking a cake," he replied.

"What does pulling on that have to do with cake?"

"It's the recipe," the Polack replied. "It said to put the batter into a bowl, then beat it for five minutes."

How can you tell if a WASP bride is really ugly?

Everyone lines up to kiss the caterer.

How can you tell if a WASP man is having a loud orgasm?

His wife wakes up.

Did you hear about the WASP whose wife died during sex?

Three and a half weeks later, he noticed.

Why are so many black men single?

It's a racial tradition—like father, like son.

What's the ASPCA?

A Polish singles bar.

How long does a JAP spend in finishing school?

Once she finds a man, she's finished.

The strong man at the state fair picked up a grapefruit in one giant hand, then squeezed. Juice poured out until the grapefruit appeared to be bone dry. The barker then announced, "Any man that can get another drop from that grapefruit wins 500 dollars."

Among the audience were several hulks from the football team at the state university. They stepped forward, then failed. Next, a group of burly construction workers took their turns with the grapefruit, but they came up dry. Two professional wrestlers suffered a similar fate.

The barker was just about to go on to the next act when a small, skinny man with thick glasses stepped forward and announced, "I want to try."

The crowd roared with laughter. Shouts of derision filled the tent as the scrawny man walked up to the table and grabbed the grapefruit. But the crowd gasped in amazement as the man squeezed a half glass of juice from the grapefruit.

The barker and the strong man came running up and demanded, "How come a wimp like you can squeeze like that?"

"I'm Jewish."

What's the primary advantage of being Polish?

You don't have to go to the zoo—the zoo comes and gets you.

Why are a Russian woman's tits like a sweet chariot?

They both swing low.

How can you tell an Italian woman in a cow pasture?

She's the one without the bell.

How do WASPs know when it's raining?

Water gets in their noses.

What's the worst advice you can give a black student?

Be yourself.

What is a Polish jigsaw puzzle?

One piece.

What happened when the Puerto Rican called the suicide hotline?

They told him he had a pretty good idea.

How can you tell a Polack's in the woods?

The bears are lighting fires to keep him away.

Why did the Polack push his baby daughter off the top of the stairs?

He wanted to watch her take her first 24 steps.

A hillbilly from the mountains of West Virginia made his first trip to New York. He checked in at the desk, then followed the desk clerk's directions toward something called an "elevator." As he ambled in that direction, he saw a very fat, very ugly old lady standing in front of a door. To the hillbilly's surprise, the door opened, the fat lady waddled inside, then the door closed.

Fascinated, the hillbilly waited patiently for the door to open again. When it did, a gorgeous young blonde sauntered out. "Gosh dang it!" the hillbilly exclaimed. "I knew I should have brought my wife!"

What's a German bigamist?

A frau loader.

Why did the Polish policeman let the Jewish criminal go?

He'd heard that Jews eat lox.

Did you hear about the Puerto Rican grade school dropout who came to New York and through hard work made himself rich, even though he only knew three words of English?

Those three words were, "Stick 'em up."

What's the basic plot of a Harlem romantic novel?

In the end, the hero gets the heroin.

One Polack said to another, "You know, my wife's the greatest cook in the world."

"How do you know?"

"Every night when I come home, there's half a dozen truck drivers eating in the kitchen."

Why do black postmen always arrive back at the post office so late?

Their roots are longer.

What's black and crisp and hangs from the ceiling?

A Polack who tried to change a light bulb.

How does a Jewish hooker get her clothes?

Hole sale.

A beggar walked up to a JAP as she was about to walk into Bloomingdale's and said, "Lady, I haven't eaten in six days."

She looked at him and said, "I wish I had your willpower."

A black athlete from Harlem was signed by a major league franchise and assigned to its farm club in Mississippi. The dude pulled into town one day in his new Corvette. He sauntered up to some white guys sitting on a bench in front of the drugstore and demanded, "Hey, Joe, where do the black dudes hang out in this town?"

The redneck eyed him, spat a wad of tobacco on the ground, then pointed. "See the big branch on that tree over there?"

What's a Jewish ménage à trois?

Two headaches and a hard-on.

Why couldn't the Polack get his computer to work?

He thought the instructions read, "Insert a floppy dick."

What's the most important thing to remember when traveling in Greece?

No matter what you drop, don't bend over!

What's the special term for raping a JAP?

Raiding the ice box.

What do you get when you come in a JAP?

Ice cream.

How do you rate screwing a JAP?

Below zero.

What's the difference between a JAP and a block of ice?

Eventually, ice melts.

What's the leading sexually transmitted disease among WASPs?

Headaches.

What does an Italian call his nose?

A snack dispenser.

Why did the Polack shout at worms?

He was trying to master bait.

What's a black kid's best subject in school?

Addiction.

Why did the Polish girl say "Stick it in my ear?"

She wanted to try aural sex.

What's a Harlem special?

Heroin, with the works.

Why did the Polack stick pins in the baked beans?

To let the gas out.

Why did the Polack throw away the toilet brush?

He went back to using paper.

Why did the horny Polack run to the department store?

He heard women's pants were half off.

What was the sign on the redneck movie theater?

Children under thirteen not admitted unless accompanied by their husbands.

Why did the bee wear a yamulka?

He wanted to make sure no one mistook him for a WASP.

Did you hear about the new Jewish tire?

It stops on a dime—and picks it up.

A JAP was out to dinner with her husband. At the end of the meal the waiter approached and asked, "Was anything all right?"

Why does a JAP close her eyes during sex?

She pretends she's shopping.

To her family's delight, the JAP landed a prize husband, the son of an English duke. After the honeymoon, the couple came to the U.S. to live. The JAP began to instruct her husband, who had grown up in a huge country estate, on more informal ways of life in the United States.

On the second day back, she took her husband to a supermarket. "Darling," she said. "I'll push this cart. You walk along and put all your favorites into the cart." He trotted off ahead of her, then returned with an armful of packages.

She inspected them, pointing. "Drop this in the cart. And this. And this." Suddenly, she spied a large steak. Her face formed an expression of deep disgust, and she said, "No. You must never buy anything like that?"

"But why?" her husband asked.

"It needs to be cooked."

Did you hear about the Polish athlete who wrapped himself in barbed wire?

He wanted to try out for fencing.

Where does an Irishman go on vacation?

To a different bar.

Why shouldn't you go to a Chinese abortionist?

30 minutes later, you're pregnant again.

Why don't JAPs exercise?

If God had wanted them to bend over, he'd have put diamonds on the floor.

Why did the Polack keep empty beer cans in the refrigerator?

For his friends who didn't drink.

What did the black guy call his pet zebra?

Spot.

How can you tell a burglar is Puerto Rican?

He knocks.

Why did the Polish sky diver die?

His snorkle didn't open.

Did you hear about the new Jewish Mother's Auto Insurance Company?

They offer a special "My Fault" policy.

Why are there so few black executives?

It's hard to get a watermelon in a briefcase.

What's another name for a Harlem housing project?

A coon-dominium.

What's the most dangerous sport in Poland?

Golf, because Polacks don't know their ass from a hole in the ground.

Why did the Polack jump through the outhouse hole?

He wanted to join the movements.

What's another name for Italian prostitutes?

Guinea pigs.

What do you get when you cross a WASP and a Mexican?

A migrant stockbroker.

The local chapter of the Ku Klux Klan purchased a huge 40-foot-tall Christmas tree. Shortly before the holiday, the Grand Dragon called the membership together to get ready for a gala celebration. "Clem," he said to one white-sheeted figure, "ya'll go down to the hardware store and get about a thousand-foot string of lights. Jake, you drive over to the hollow and buy a few jugs of moonshine. The Carter brothers, you two slaughter a hog for the barbeque, and Jenkins, you split some wood for the fire."

The men named scurried off. The rest sat for a moment. Then one asked, "Boss, what do we do?"

The Grand Dragon replied, "I want you to go out and invite twenty niggers to the party."

"Niggers?" the Klansman scoffed. "Why do we need niggers?"

"When you got a tree that big," the Grand Dragon replied, "you need ornaments."

The WASP freshman girl was taking a walk around the Harvard campus with her roommate, a black girl from Harlem. They spotted a very preppy upperclassman walking their way. The WASP turned to her roommate and gushed, "Oh, I just love a man with a pipe, don't you?"

"No way," the black girl replied. "I loves them with my pussy."

The black dude walked into the house to see his wife dancing seductively in front of him. "Hey, babe," he said, "where'd you get that grass skirt?"

"That ain't no grass skirt," she replied. "I had my hair straightened."

It was the guy's first day at the sex aids store. His very first customer was a white woman, who asked about the price of dildos. The man replied, "Well, I've got this sleek white Warren Beatty model for $39.95 and this big black Mike Tyson model for $49.95." The girl buys the black dildo and leaves.

The second customer was a black chick, also looking for a self-amusement rod. The salesman offers her the same models, but switches the price. Sure enough, the black girl goes for the white model.

Proud of himself, he moved on to his third customer, a Polish girl who also asked to see dildos. The salesman said, "I've got this white one at $39.95, this black one at $49.95, and this red one at $79.95." The Polish girl took the red one, paid, and left the store.

A couple minutes later, the store owner walked in and asked the salesman, "How's business?"

"Pretty good," the guy said, "I sold a white one, a black one, and the fire extinguisher."

Why did the Polack cut the legs off his cow?

He wanted ground beef.

Did you hear about the Polish mime troupe?

They talk.

How can you tell a Polack in a casino?

He's playing the stamp machine.

The woman had just arrived in New York when a Puerto Rican dude came up to her and asked, "Hey, you know where Central Park is?"

"I'm afraid not," the woman replied.

The Puerto Rican said, "Okay, I'll rape you here."

Did you hear about the new Lebanese toilet paper?

It blows your shit away.

What's black, has white eyes, and knocks on glass?

A black kid in a microwave.

Why don't blacks and hispanics intermarry?

Their kids would be too lazy to steal.

Why are so many Italian men named Tony?

Because when they arrived on the boat, their foreheads were stamped, "To N.Y."

Why did the Italian get fired from his job cleaning toilets in a Las Vegas casino?

They caught him skimming off the top.

Why do blacks have such big nostrils?

Because their fingers are big.

How does a Polack take a shower?

He pees in a fan.

Did you hear about the Polish college student who thought she was a robot because she was made by a scientist?

Why aren't there any black sky divers?

Their lips explode at 1,500 feet.

Why did the Polack lose his girlfriend?

He forgot where he laid her.

A woman walked next door to see her Jewish neighbor, Mrs. Cohen. She found the lady carefully scraping the paint off the living-room wall and collecting the chips in a cup. The woman asked, "Mrs. Cohen, are you going to repaint?"

"No," Mrs. Cohen replied. "We're moving."

How do you know a Russian girl is fat?

She sprays oil and vinegar on the lawn, then grazes.

Did you hear about the Polack who made counterfeit 2-dollar bills?

He took twenties, then erased the zeros.

One guy said to another, "I read that the Polish space agency has announced plans to send a man to the sun."

The second guy said, "That's stupid. He'll burn up."

"No, he won't," the first man said. "They're going to send him at night."

Why did the deaf Polack stick condoms in his ears?

He didn't want to get hearing aids.

Why do single Polish guys hang out in the hen-house?

They heard it was a good place to pick up chicks.

What's a Puerto Rican vacation:

Buying a six-pack and hanging out on your neighbor's stoop.

What's different about little black girls?

They was ate before they was seven.

Did you hear about the ugly Polish baby?

His mother took the placenta home.

What did the Jewish guy do when he discovered that his girlfriend had a heart of gold?

Ripped it out and sold it.

Why did the Polack give his wife a wig for Christmas?

His neighbor told him she was getting balled every day.

What's the book of fairy tales for black kids?

Motherfucker Goose.

What's the difference between a Jewish American Princess and an Italian American Princess?

With an Italian American Princess, the jewels are fake and the orgasms are real.

How did the Polack get killed at the Halloween Party?

He was bobbing for apples and someone flushed.

Why are there nude pictures of black women?

So gorillas can masturbate.

One Polack was admiring another's footwear. He asked, "What kind of shoes are those?"

The second Polack said, "These are my Italian shoes."

"How do you know they're Italian shoes?"

"Because everywhere I go, dago."

What do you get when you cross an Irishman and a Jew?

A drunk who gets his liquor wholesale.

How do Jews celebrate Christmas?

They put a parking meter on the roof.

Chapter Two

Gross Celebrity Jokes

What do you call people who don't believe in astrology?

Democrats.

One guy at a bar turned to his buddy and said, "You know, I like Ronald Reagan a lot better than George Bush."

The other guy said, "I think they're the same. Both of them say absolutely nothing."

"Yeah," the first guy admitted. "But when Reagan says nothing, you know he really means it."

What's the difference between the movie star's hair and her lover?

Both of them are blown dry every day.

How bad is inflation?

So bad that if you drop a dollar on the street, you get a ticket for littering.

What do the Virgin Mary and Mary Beth Whitehead have in common?

They were both surrogate mothers.

Why do Ron and Nancy Reagan look so tired?

They're suffering from a bad case of AIDES.

How thin is Nancy Reagan?

Well, they sent her picture to Ethiopia, and Ethiopians sent back food.

What's the motto of the U.S. Navy in the Persian Gulf?

"Kill them all. Let God sort them out."

A deputy came in and told the Ayatollah Khomeni about the U.S. shooting down an Iranian airbus. The Ayatollah was furious. "Those infidels!" he swore. "Killing innocent men, women, and children. Who do they think they are, me?"

How do we know Abe Lincoln was Jewish?

He was shot in the temple.

How did the movie star do in the Hollywood Blow Job Contest?

She won by six laps.

Why is the movie star like a Tootsie Roll?

They're both terrific suckers.

Did you hear that George Bush abuses his wife?

He stays married to her.

Why did Dan Quayle do so badly in school?

The only letter he bothered learning was "I".

Why does Dan Quayle enjoy having a cold?

It's the only thing he can keep in his head for more than a minute.

Why did Moses get such a leading role in the Bible?

When he was discovered, he looked good in the rushes.

How did Mike Tyson meet Robin Givens?

One day he opened his wallet, and there she was.

Did you hear that Boy George had sex with a member of the Royal Family?

Rumor has it he had Prince Albert in his can.

How can you tell if Prince Charles is horny?

He's got a stiff upper lip.

What's the worst thing about being a University of Oklahoma football player?

Your parents keep writing you for money.

Why was the Reagan administration like cocktail party refreshments?

They both consisted of an assortment of nuts.

The British Royal Family was on safari in Kenya and had camped for the night in the bush. One of the guides was assigned to keep guard. Some time after midnight, the guide heard a thrashing near a big tent. He rushed off, and a few minutes later several shots were heard.

When the guide returned to the campfire, Prince Philip was waiting for him. "Tell me, my good man," the prince inquired, "what was that commotion about?"

"I heard a noise," the guide replied. "When I went to investigate, I saw the outline of this horrible figure with broad shoulders, an equine face, and an enormous rear end. So I aimed and fired several times."

"My God, man!" the prince exclaimed. "You've shot the queen!"

A newspaper reporter asked Dolly Parton how long it took to get her hair done.

She replied, "I don't know. I'm never there."

How boring was the last presidential election?

When voters walked into the booth and pulled the lever, the machine yawned.

How cold was it last winter?

So cold Elizabeth Taylor almost got married again.

Why is Dan Quayle like Indiana State Highway 131?

They both have a big yellow stripe down the middle.

What's the difference between Jane Fonda and Dan Quayle?

Jane Fonda spent more time in Vietnam.

Why did George Bush select Dan Quayle as his running mate?

When you go fishing for votes, you need a worm.

Why was Oedipus's mother mad at him?

He was hard on her.

How did the golfer's wife help him straighten out his putter?

She licked his balls.

Why is Dan Quayle like a skeleton?

Neither one has any guts.

Did you hear about the new Tammy Faye Bakker made-up kit?

It comes with three gallon cans and an ice-cream scoop.

Why was Robin Givens always black and blue?

Mike Tyson knocked before he entered.

Why is sprinter Ben Johnson like an archeologist?

His career lies in ruins.

Did you hear that Imelda Marcos committed suicide?

She piled up all her clothes, then jumped.

Why did Donald Duck ditch Daisy?

He got tired of her quack.

High on a lonely mountain in Switzerland, a brilliant but insane modern scientist spent his lifetime trying to bring to life the fictional dream of Dr. Frankenstein. After decades of perfecting his technique, he sent his assistant to comb the world for the finest body parts. Slowly he collected the mind of a Nobel Prize-winning physicist, the heart and lungs of a marathon runner, the legs of a champion bodybuilder, the face of a Robert Redford look-alike.

Finally the great day was at hand. But just before he was to bring his creation to life, his assistant said, "Dr. Gottfried, there's one thing missing." The startled scientist replied, "What could it be?" The assistant whispered in his ear.

The doctor inspected his creation, sighed, then said, "You're right. My work must be complete. I want you to go out into the world and come back with the perfect asshole."

Three days later, the assistant came back to the lab with Dan Quayle.

What do you call it when Gloria Steinem goes to the bathroom?

A feminist movement.

What do you call it when Ralph Nader goes to the bathroom?

A consumer movement.

What do you call it when the pope goes to the bathroom?

A religious movement.

The movie star was recuperating in a private suite at the hospital. Her doctor walked in to check on her, and she asked, "Doctor, darling, I must know. How long will it be before I can have sex again?"

"I really can't say," the doctor replied. "No one's ever asked me that after a tonsilectomy."

Why is President Reagan like a high-class Washington call girl?

He's slept with nearly every important Republican—only he did it at Cabinet meetings.

What's the movie star?

Living proof that women are never satisfied.

What's the difference between baseball and politics?

In baseball, if you're caught stealing, you're out.

What's this? [Hold up a blank sheet of paper?]

Dan Quayle's essay on "What I Would Do As President."

Why do Republicans give such good head?

They'll swallow anything.

Did you hear about George Bush's plan to solve our biggest urban problem?

It's called "AIDS for the Homeless."

Weren't Robin Givens and Mike Tyson a fastidious couple?

She's fast and he's hideous.

Why does Ronald Reagan call Nancy "Mummy" when they're in bed?

She's dry as dust and hasn't moved in 2,000 years.

What happened when Tammy Faye Bakker scraped off all her makeup?

They discovered that underneath she was Jimmy Hoffa.

How bad is Ronald Reagan's memory?

Last week he forgot the Alamo.

What's so distinctive about the movie star's ass?

It has more fingerprints than the FBI.

What's Jim Bakker's new commandment?

"Thou shalt use thy rod on thine staff."

What's the difference between a Republican woman and a Democratic woman?

A Republican woman has Bush in her heart, and a Democratic woman has Hart in her bush.

Did you hear about the new Donna Rice medicine?

It's a Hart stimulant.

What does George Burns mean when he complains about not getting enough action?

His prune juice isn't working.

Did you hear that when Jesse Jackson became successful, he decided to help his family by hiring his mother to clean his house?

Unfortunately, he had to fire her because she stole.

What was the worst mistake Gary Hart made with Donna Rice?

Not letting Ted Kennedy drive her home.

What's the definition of "redundant?"

Telling Ronald Reagan to "forget it."

What did Rock Hudson and King Henry the VIII have in common?

They both screwed queens and died.

If Tarzan were Puerto Rican, what would Cheetah be?

Pregnant.

If Tarzan and Jane were Jewish, what would Cheetah be?

A fur coat.

Chapter 3

Gross Animal Jokes

Why is a roving tomcat like a desperate poker player?

They both put everything they have into the kitty.

The little girl walked into the kitchen and said, "Mommy, can I have some birdseed?"

"Certainly," her mother said. She took the package from the cupboard and handed a cupful to the little girl.

The little girl took the cup, then walked over and placed it in front of the family cat.

"Megan," the mother scolded. "You know better than that. The birdseed is for our parakeet. Why are you feeding it to the cat."

Megan replied. "Because that's where the parakeet is."

After the egg hunt on Easter Sunday, the young farm boy decided to play a prank. He went to the chicken coop and replaced every single egg with a brightly colored one.

A few minutes later the rooster walked in, saw all the eggs, then stormed outside and killed the peacock.

The male robin flew into the nest one day. He took a look, then demanded, "How did this one speckled egg get there?"

The female robin replied, "I did it for a lark."

Desperate for employment, a man took a job on a ranch in a remote area of Australia. The work was hard and the social life nonexistent. Finally, after two solid weeks of labor, the foreman announced that a wagonload of beer would be available that evening.

The man wanted female company more than a drink, but one beer led to another. Soon everything was a blur. The next thing he knew, another ranchhand was shaking him awake. When he tried to move, he realized he'd never felt worse in his life. His head was pounding, he stank to high heaven, and his dick was so sore he couldn't touch it.

"Come on," the other hand said, "It's time to tend

the sheep."

"Fuck the sheep," the man said crossly.

"No, not now," the other hand said. "Didn't you fuck enough of them last night?"

One cat was walking by the tennis courts one day when he saw another cat sitting there, staring intently at the action. The first cat went up to his friend and said, "Hey, what do you think you're doing? We cats don't like tennis."

The second cat replied, "Oh, I'm not interested in tennis myself. But my father's in the racket."

What did the cat do after he ate cheese?

Put his mouth over the mouse hole, then waited with baited breath.

How do you tell a boy sardine from a girl sardine?

You wait and see which can they come out of.

A guy walked into a bar in a tough New York neighborhood pulling a big, mangy-looking yellow dog. He ordered a shot and a beer, then began bragging how tough his dog was.

The bartender listened to the guy for a few minutes, then got fed up. He went in the back room and came back with a ferocious, growling pit bull. He said to the guy, "A hundred bucks says my pit bull will make mincemeat of your mutt."

The guy agreed. They went into the back room and let the animals loose. To the astonishment of the bartender, the yellow dog just tore the pit bull apart, then ate the entire animal. He turned to the owner and asked, "What in the hell kind of dog is that?"

"Don't know," the guy said. "A friend sent him to me from Africa. All I did was cut off his big mane and his tail."

A little Vietnamese boy walked into a pet store with an elderly man who approached the store owner and said something to him in Vietnamese. The little boy translated, "My grandfather say he want to buy a dog for me."

The store owner beamed. "Why, that's terrific." He showed them to a row of cages in the back of the store. "How about this adorable little puppy here?"

The boy translated for his grandfather, who replied. Then the boy turned to the store owner and said, "Grandfather says that one is too little."

"Ah, you want an older dog," the owner said. He walked to another cage and pointed out a collie. "How about this one? He'll run forever." The boy and the grandfather consulted, then the boy said, "Grandfather say this one too skinny."

The store owner thought for a moment. Then he led the way to a Labrador retriever. "This is the dog for you. He's friendly, gentle. Plus, he can sit up, beg, roll over, stand on his hind legs, and fetch anything you throw."

The boy and his grandfather talked again. Then the boy said to the store owner, "Grandfather say forget about the tricks. Is the dog tender?"

A man walked into the biggest clothing store in town and bragged, "I'm the world's best salesman. Give me a job."

The owner of the store replied, "Sorry. I don't have any openings."

The salesman asked, "How many suits does your best salesman sell in a day?"

"About ten."

"I guarantee to double that total today. And I'll work without pay."

The store owner decided he could hardly lose in that deal. He nodded his agreement, then went back into his office. When he came out at 5:00 o'clock, he was astonished to find that the salesman had sold 21 suits. "Now do I get the job?"

The owner thought for a moment, then said, "I'll hire you if you do one more thing." He went back in the storeroom, then returned with the ugliest suit in the world, a model with violently clashing purple and yellow stripes. The owner told the salesman, "You've got to sell this suit by closing tonight."

The owner barely had been back in his office for half an hour when the salesman came in and brashly handed him a receipt for the ugly suit. The owner said, "Well, you're hired. But tell me one thing—how did you convince a customer to buy that suit?"

"Convincing the customer was easy," the salesman replied. "Strangling his seeing-eye dog was the nasty part."

Where do sheep get sheared?

At the baaaa-baaaa shop.

A Wall Street wheeler and dealer was fishing one day in the middle of a lake when he hauled in a very unusual-looking fish. The business tycoon took the fish off the line, then dropped him on the bottom of the boat. The fish wiggled in agony, then, to the man's amazement, said, "I am a magic fish. If you throw me back in the lake, I'll give you three wishes."

Visions of becoming a multi-billionaire flashed

through the Wall Streeter's mind. But instinct took over and he said, "Fish, I need five wishes."

The fish continued to flop and struggle. Then it gasped, "Only three wishes."

"God damn it," the businessman swore. "You take me for a sucker. How about four and a half wishes?"

The fish stammered. "Three wishes. Only three wishes."

The businessman was steaming because he prided himself on always getting the better deal. He paced back and forth, furious. Finally he convinced himself that three wishes were enough to give him everything he ever wanted out of life. He turned back to the fish and conceded, "Okay, fish, I'll take the three wishes."

But the fish was dead.

A man walked into a newspaper office and told the girl in the classified department, "I want to put an ad in the paper. My wife's cat is missing and I'm offering a $10,000 reward."

The girl was shocked. "Isn't that an enormous amount of money for a cat?"

The guy grinned. "No, it isn't. I drowned the cat yesterday."

Did you hear about the flock of macho eagles in Idaho?

They all had pictures of sailors tatooed on their breasts.

Did you hear about the chicken who ate a copy of the *Daily Racing Form?*

The next day, she was laying odds.

What do you get when you cross a turkey and an ostrich?

A Thanksgiving dish that hides its head in the mashed potatoes.

Why did the leopard get so frustrated?

He couldn't find the right spot.

What's the difference between an old cat and a kitten?

An old cat scratches and claws, but a little pussy never hurt anybody.

How do you make an elephant fly?

First, you get a huge zipper.

Why do little rabbits love going to school?

That's where they learn to multiply.

What's must reading for the modern shepherd?

"AIDS and Ewe"

Did you hear about the guy who crossed Alaska by sled team?

By the time he got home, he was a real husky fucker.

A duck walked into a brothel and announced, "I want a hooker right away.

The madam said, "Certainly. Will that be cash?"

"No," said the duck. "Put her on my bill."

What do you call it when two chickens fool around?

Fowl play.

Did you hear about the new Scottish porno movie?

Sheep Throat.

How do you know your dog is gay?

He lays his paw on the table.

Why is it a mistake to fuck a pig?

It'll squeal on you.

What's the difference between a pussy and a cunt?

A pussy is soft and furry and warm. A cunt is what owns it.

Chapter Four

Gross Homosexual Jokes

Why do gays hate movies about AIDS?

They always get it in the end.

Did you hear about the new French vegetables that eat each other?

They're called "Les Beans"

Why don't gays play chess?

Because every once in a while, a chess player has to sacrifice a queen.

What's a mixed marriage in San Francisco?

The husband and wife are of the opposite sex.

What weighs 500 pounds and swims in San Francisco Bay?

Moby Dyke.

Two gays met on the street and one said, "Darling, I haven't seen Bruce in ages. Do you know where he is?"

The other gay shook his head slowly. "I'm afraid he's no longer with us. He went on a safari in Africa and was eaten by a lion."

"How awful!"

"Actually," the second fag added, "he loved every minute of it."

What word does every flaming faggot pronounce wrong?

Wrong.

How do gays decide which condom to buy?

They put one over a candle, then sit on it.

What's a gay's favorite toast?

"Bottoms up!"

Why is a 25-year-old faggot like a 90-year-old heterosexual?

For each one, sex is behind him.

Why did the lesbian say no when the two lady athletes wanted to screw her?

She demanded separate Czechs.

How do you tell the gay Arabs?

They're dancing sheik to sheik.

What was the most popular booth at the San Francisco street fair?

"Guess Your Sex—25 cents"

Why do faggots love a hamburger?

Because it's hot meat between two buns.

Why didn't the gay snob like sodomy?

Any ass can do it.

How do you know a grocery store's owned by a faggot?

All the meat is in cans.

What did the very horny faggot do when he saw the blind man begging on the street?

He made a deposit in his can.

Why do gays like Thanksgiving?

They can go out and look for a gobbler.

Why was the gay sergeant court-martialed?

They caught him playing with his privates.

What does the sign read in the locker room of the woman's tennis tour?

"If you beat me, you can eat me."

Why don't women tennis pros get into fights on the court?

They get their licks in in the shower room.

What's life on the women's tennis tour like?

You muff a few strokes on the court, then stroke a few muffs in the locker room.

How do you know a bus driver's gay?

He directs you to the rear.

How can you tell if a guy is gay?

He's got crabs in his eyebrows.

One faggot ran into another and said, "George, you look awful."

"I feel awful, darling," the second fag said. "I've got lesions all over my body, I'm losing weight, and I spend all day and all night coughing."

"What did the doctor say?"

"He said it must be someone I ate."

How can you tell a guy is gay?

If you ask him to have a bite, he gets down on his knees.

What happens the first time you walk into a gay bar?

You feel a little queer.

How do gays keep from getting AIDS?

They beat it off.

What do you call a naked faggot with a hard-on?

A can opener.

What do most gays get for Christmas these days?

Buried.

What's the definition of an optimist?

A faggot with an IRA.

What should you do if you're terrified of getting AIDS?

Get ahold of yourself.

Why is a gay like Mount St. Helens?

An eruption could be fatal.

What's the difference between a thorn and a homosexual?

A thorn pricks your finger, and . . .

Why did the gay have feathers in his mouth?

He finally found a safe cock to suck.

How do you tell a heterosexual from a homosexual?

A heterosexual likes to eat out; a homosexual prefers to brown bag it.

How are gays born?

By C-suction.

What's a lesbian?

A woman trying to do a man's job.

What's the difference between a straight rodeo and a gay rodeo?

At the straight rodeo, they yell, "Ride that sucker!"

What's the most popular line in a gay bar?

"Mind if I push your stool in?"

What's the difference between a straight woman and a lesbian?

A straight woman loves a big prick, while a lesbian prefers the box it comes in.

Why are most butchers gay?

They take their meat in the back.

What's the difference between Greenwich Village and Staten Island?

Staten Island has ferry terminals, Greenwich Village has terminal ferries.

What's the number of the AIDS Hotline?

1-800-BUT-FUCK

What's a .38 caliber Smith & Wesson?

The cure for AIDS.

Why is there so little cocksucking in San Francisco these days?

Most of the fruits are rotting.

Chapter Five

A Gross Variety

Did you hear about the three cannibals who captured a school bus?

Two days later, they passed the entire class.

A cannibal went to the witch doctor to complain that he felt weak and dizzy all the time. The witch doctor asked the cannibal if there had been any changes in his diet recently.

"Well," the cannibal said, "we did capture a dozen shipwrecked sailors last week."

"Ah," the witch doctor said. "You've probably got high blood pressure. So you're going to cut way down on your consumption of salts."

Little Johnny brought to school a box wrapped with a red ribbon as a present for his teacher. He handed it to her. She started to guess what was inside.

"Chocolates?" she asked.

"Nope."

"A cake?"

Johnny shook his head no.

Then the teacher noticed some liquid dripping from the corner of the box. She caught a few drops on her finger, put the finger in her mouth, then said, "Ah, I know—dill pickles."

"No," Johnny said. "It's a puppy."

A cannibal walked into the village to find a man dressed in a gray flannel suit and carrying a briefcase steaming in a pot of boiling water. He turned to the cook and complained, "Oh, no, not another businessman's special."

THE WORLD'S OLDEST CANNIBAL JOKE

A cannibal wife stormed up to her husband and demanded, "Who was that lady I saw you with last night?"

The husband replied, "That was no lady, that was my dinner."

Why was the cannibal fired from his job?

He was caught buttering up his boss.

What did the cannibal say when he saw two hunters in a Jeep?

"Meals on Wheels!"

Why did Dracula sprinkle grass seed in his hair?

"Because I vant to be a lawn."

What was printed on the road sign in cannibal country?

"Take the bus, and leave the driver to us."

What do they serve in a cannibal deli?

Him on rye.

Why should you always be late to a cannibal dinner?

Because their rule is, "First come, first served."

Why was the cannibal so excited when his wife became pregnant?

Until then, he didn't know where his next meal was coming from.

Why is an Arab like a cannibal?

If you get either one a date, they'll eat it.

Why did the cannibal offer cocaine to the cop who arrested him?

He wanted to appeal to a higher authority.

What do you call a man who's still got his appendix and tonsils?

Doctor.

An actress flew to Europe to begin work on a new film. A few weeks later she sent a telegram to her psychiatrist:

"Having a wonderful time. Why?"

Why was the gynecologist unemployed?

He couldn't find any openings.

Why is it great to be a gynecologist?

Who else can order a woman to take off her clothes and spread her legs, leisurely inspect her most intimate parts, then send the bill to her husband?

Chapter Six

Gross Religious Jokes

What's black and white and black and white and black and white and black and white and black and white and black and white and black and white and black and white and black and white?

A nun falling down the stairs.

What's black and white and has a hole in the middle?

A nun.

What's Jim Bakker's favorite Christmas carol?

"Cum, All Ye Faithful."

What's Jim Bakker's favorite religious activity?

Laying on of hands.

How do you make holy water?

Take some tap water, and boil the hell out of it.

Two slightly inebriated Irishmen arrived at the door of the convent late on Friday evening. They banged loudly until a nun opened the door. They told the nun that they had to speak with the Mother Superior about a very urgent matter.

The Reverend Mother was summoned. One Irishman removed his hat respectfully, then asked, "Excuse me, Your Holiness, but do you have any midget nuns in this convent?"

"Why, no, we do not," she replied. The two men whispered for a moment, then the first asked, "Sister, do you know of any midget nuns in any of the neighboring parishes?"

Again, the reply was negative. The two men whispered once more, then the man asked, "If I could ask one more question, Reverend Mother—do you know of any midget nuns in the whole of Ireland?"

"No, I do not."

The first man turned, slapped the other across the face, then shouted, "I told you, dummy, you fucked a penguin!"

A priest and rabbi were sitting next to each other on an airplane when the captain announced that they were having engine trouble. He went on to add that they were about to enter a thunderstorm, and he cautioned the passengers to say their last prayers.

Immediately, the priest fell to his knees, made the sign of the cross, and began to pray. Out of the corner of his eye, he was astounded to see the rabbi do the same set of motions. For a few moments, his safety was on his mind as the plane pitched and dipped. When they reached smoother air, the priest turned to the rabbi and said, "So, I caught you. When you thought you were to pass beyond, you turned to the Lord Jesus for solace?"

"Not at all," the rabbi replied. "I just made the standard checks—spectacles, testicles, money, cigars."

One black walking down the street greeted another with, "Hey, mothafucka."

The other replied, "Morning, Reverend."

Are TV evangelists all sex maniacs?

No, each just wants to experience the glory of his coming.

Why are TV evangelists so valuable?

Few people really knew what sin was until they came along and showed them.

Why is Jimmy Swaggart like a hog farmer?

They both pay 50 dollars for a pig.

Why did Jessica Hahn lose faith in Jim Bakker?

When there turned out to be no Second Coming.

How can you tell a really horny nun?

She's the one with the vibrating crucifix.

What did the bishop do when the young priest confessed he was so horny that he was constantly aroused?

Got down on his knees, offered a prayer to God, then licked the problem.

Why do priests have no problem believing in the Holy spirit?

Most of them are fairies.

How do you know a priest is gay?

After mass, he asks for donations in the rear.

Do priests start right out fucking nuns?

No, it usually takes them a while to get into the habit.

Why did Judas kiss Jesus?

To make sure it was him who was hung.

What do gay priests do in their spare time?

Memorize a new him.

Why are there so few Polish monks?

The vow of silence includes farting.

What happens when a priest gets an overwhelming attraction for a man?

He gets defrocked.

When a Catholic makes the sign of the cross, what's he most thankful for?

That they crucified Christ instead of castrating him.

Chapter Seven

Gross Senior Citizen Jokes

How can you tell if your wife's got AIDS or Alzheimer's Disease?

Take her out in the woods and leave her. If she comes home, don't fuck her.

What's the difference between the young and the old?

The young don't know what to do, and the old can no longer do what they know.

Why are the Super Bowl champs like an 80-year-old bridegroom?

They're both on top for a year.

Mr. Simpson, a bookkeeper by profession, lived with his mother for the first 61 years of his life. She finally passed away at age 84. Six months later, to the surprise of everyone who knew him, Mr. Simpson announced his engagement.

The wedding took place shortly afterward, and the couple went off on their honeymoon. Charlie, Simpson's neighbor, came over to the house shortly after their return. Curious, he got the very meek and proper bookkeeper aside and whispered, "So, Simpson, how did you find it?"

Simpson blushed, then replied, "With difficulty."

"What do you mean, with difficulty?"

Simpson leaned over and whispered, "Who would have thought to look under all that hair?"

Where do most spinsters get their first date?

On their tombstones.

Everybody snickered when the 81-year-old banker married the 24-year-old chorus girl. The morning after the ceremony, nearly half the town managed to be in the vicinity of the hotel where the couple spent their first night. To everyone's astonishment, however, the old geezer sauntered out of the hotel spry as a teenager, while his young bride, haggard and bedraggled, could barely walk.

A woman rushed up to the chorus girl and said, "What happened to you?"

The buxom blonde turned and replied, "When he told me he'd been saving it up for sixty years, I thought he meant money!"

What did the World War I vet sing to his penis before he masturbated?

"The Yanks are coming, the Yanks are coming."

Why are old people so wrinkled?

Ever try to iron one?

The white-haired man, obviously in his seventies, paced nervously back and forth in the hospital waiting room. Finally a nurse came out and told him that his 24-year-old wife had just delivered twins.

A huge grin came to the face of the elderly gentleman. He puffed out his chest and bragged, "That'll show all those people who laughed when we got married. There may be snow on my roof, but there's still a raging fire in my furnace."

The nurse replied, "There may be a fire, but I'd advise you to clean the soot out of your chimney—both babies are black."

Two old women were sitting on the bench talking when one asked the other, "How's your husband holding up in bed these days?"

The second old woman replied, "He makes me feel like an exercise bike."

"How's that?"

"He climbs on and starts pumping away, but we never get anywhere."

An old man and an old woman were driving down the road when a cop car pulled up behind them and flashed its lights. The old man pulled over and stopped the car. The policeman approached and said, "Roll down the window, Pop."

The old lady, who was very hard of hearing, asked, "What's he saying?" The old man shouted, "He said he wants the window down." Then he rolled down the window.

"You were speeding," the cop explained.

"What'd he say?" the old lady asked.

"He said we were speeding."

The policeman then asked, "Where are you from?"

The old lady shouted, "What'd he say?"

"He wants to know where we live," the old man said. He turned to the traffic officer and said, "We're from New Jersey."

"I was there once," the cop said. "I had the worst lay of my life in New Jersey."

"What'd he say?" the old lady asked.

The old man replied, "He says he knows you."

An old woman was growing weaker by the hour, and the doctor held out little hope. Her husband knelt by her bedside, praying as she slept. Finally the old woman awoke and her husband asked, "Gloria, is there anything else I can do for you?"

"Well, there is one thing," Gloria replied weakly. "In 46 years of marriage, we never had anal intercourse. Can we do it before I die?"

The thought made the old man shudder, but he dropped his pants, rolled her over, and climbed aboard. Afterward they both fell asleep. The next morning, to his amazement, he awoke to the sound of his wife singing. He walked into the kitchen to see her dancing around the room while she cooked a huge breakfast. "I feel wonderful," she exclaimed. "I called the doctor and he said I'm cured."

Suddenly the old man started to sob. Gloria went to him and asked, "What's the matter? Aren't you happy I'm alive?"

"Yes," the old man said tearfully. "But I can't help thinking, if only I'd known. Papa and Mama would still be alive!"

The old maid walked into the butcher shop and ordered a salami. The butcher put it in on the machine and began slicing. The old maid yelled, "Hey, what do you think I am, a slot machine?"

Chapter Eight

Gross Sex Jokes

The rookie on the police force was sitting on a stool in the local hangout after his first day on patrol. His partner, a veteran, had spent the day introducing him to people on his beat. The two were on their second beers when a young woman with a great body walked into the bar.

"Wow," the rooky exclaimed. He turned to his partner and asked, "Who is that?"

"I don't know her real name," the partner replied. "Everybody refers to her as 911."

"911? What does that mean?"

"Every time she gets a call, a cop comes."

What's reality?

An illusion produced by a severe alcohol deficiency.

A beautiful woman was sitting at the poolside bar at the Caribbean resort when a guy came up next to her. He ordered a drink, turned, inspected her from head to toe, then said, "You know, I really love to travel."

She grunted, trying to ignore him.

Arrogantly, he put his arm around her shoulders and said, "And you know what? I also love sex. What do you say to that?"

The woman turned to him and said, "You really love sex and travel?"

"Yeah."

"Then go take a fucking hike."

One woman was complaining to her friend, "My sex life is awful. My husband doesn't have the foggiest idea what it takes to get me to come. What's worse, he gets really mad when I try to tell him."

"Do what I did," her friend replied. "I told my husband that I was exactly like his computer."

"Like his computer?"

"Yeah," the second woman replied. "We both come with instructions."

What's an optimist?

A guy who thinks his wife has finally given up cigarettes when he finds cigar butts around the house.

Why is a high-class hooker like a defense contractor?

They both charge 100 dollars for a screw.

Why did all the young girls flock to the courtroom?

They'd heard about the hung jury.

Why is sex like life insurance?

The older you get, the more it costs.

Three guys were sitting at the bar. The first guy said, "You know, I'm really lucky. When my wife makes love, she's like an acrobat. She can get into the most incredible positions."

The second guy said, "I'm lucky, too. My wife is

like a world-class pianist when we have sex. She's got the most talented hands you can imagine."

No one spoke for a moment. Then the first guy said to the third guy, "George, how's your wife in bed?"

George took a sip of his beer, then replied, "I guess you could say that my wife makes love like a chess player."

"A chess player?"

"Yeah. Every twenty minutes, she moves."

The gorgeous blond streetwalker staggered into the precinct house, complaining that she'd been dragged into an alley, stripped of all her clothes, and brutally raped. She was escorted into the office of a handsome young detective.

The sight of the gorgeous hunk revived the hooker's spirits. He was more than a little interested after a view of her curves. One thing led to another, and soon they were rolling around on the floor.

Suddenly the door opened and the precinct captain walked in. When he saw what was going on, he barked, "Creskin, what in the hell is going on? You're supposed to be investigating a rape."

The detective sat up and replied, "Uh, Captain, I was just reconstructing the crime."

Did you hear about the guy whose asthma turned him into a sex maniac?

He discovered he could only catch his breath in snatches.

The guy walked into the bar looking like he'd been run over by a truck. His hair was matted, his face bloody and scratched, his clothes torn. His friends bought him a beer, then asked, "What happened?"

The guy chugged the beer and said, "I was fighting for Joanne's virginity?"

"No kidding?"

"Yeah. But that little tiger was determined to keep it."

Did you hear about the condoms with the little yellow signs?

The signs read, "Baby on Board."

Two guys were talking at the bar when the door to the establishment opened. A tall, athletic-looking man walked in. Immediately three girls came over and took his arm. One guy said to the other,

"Who's that?"

"He's the quarterback for the Giants," the guy explained.

The first guy said, "The guy who signed the 5-million-dollar contract? No wonder the girls are after him."

The two guys continued to drink for a moment. Then the door opened and a tall slender black guy walked in. Immediately four girls were all over him. The first guy pointed and asked, "Who's that?"

"The starting center on the Knicks," the second guy explained.

The first guy said, "I've heard those guys are hung. No wonder he's got four girls."

They drank for a moment. Then the door opened. In walked a short, fat guy who was nearly bald. Two dozen gorgeous girls immediately sprinted for the door, nearly trampling everyone else in the bar.

The first guy watched in amazement, then asked, "Who the hell is that?"

"Freddie Jones. He's a plasterer on that new building down the street."

"A plasterer?" the first guy exclaimed. "Why the hell are all those girls going after him?"

"Because," the second guy explained, "plasterers really know how to fill a crack."

Why is a nymphomaniac like a doorknob?

Everybody gets a turn.

What's the hardest thing for a woman to do on her wedding night?

Say "ouch" like she means it.

Why is your wife like a turtle?

She's slow, wrinkled, and can't get off her back.

What's the most important question to ask if you're interested in safe sex?

"Exactly what time will your husband be home?"

Where does a hooker write her memoirs?

In a loose-life notebook.

Why did the gynecologist stop practicing medicine to become a comedian?

After so many years, he decided he wanted to see men crack up.

Why are so many gynecologists treated for depression?

They spend every day feeling low.

Name three things the average husband can do in three minutes?

Drain a can of beer, belch, and make love to his wife.

Why is the Panama Canal like a hooker?

They're both very busy ditches.

Why is it so much fun to dance at a nudist colony?

You can see exactly what you're up against.

What did the Indian say to the mermaid?

How?

How do scientists tell male chromosomes from female chromosomes?

They look inside their genes.

Did you hear about the new correspondence course in sex?

You invite the mailman in.

How does an elk make love?

How should I know, I'm a Rotarian myself.

What do you call people who screw in an airplane lavatory?

Flexible fliers.

Why don't they serve whiskey sours on airplanes?

You'll never find a stewardess with a cherry.

Why did the nymphomaniac buy a nightgown with fur around the hemline?

To keep her neck warm.

How do you get to be the head cheerleader?

Take an oral exam.

Why is a hooker like a movie theater?

You pay before you enter.

A man said to his friend on the train one morning, "I kicked Helen out of the house last night."

"Why?" the friend asked.

"She was screwing her riding instructor."

"How do you know?" the friend inquired.

"I went down to the stable one day," the first man

said. "When they came back from their ride, it dawned on me why they were winded and the horses weren't."

"Boy oh boy, what a night!" the man exclaimed as he sat down next to his friend on the bus. "I came home from work, opened the door, and the scent of her perfume was all over the house. I knew she was ready for action."

The other man replied, "One sniff tells me when I'm going to get to screw my wife, too."

"Perfume?" the first man asked.

His friend shook his head. "Lysol."

A man slumped into his seat on the train. His friend noticed his sour expression and asked, "Fred, what's wrong?"

"Last night, while I was paying the bills, I finally got fed up with the way Mabel throws money around. So I stormed into the living room and gave her a lecture about economy."

"Get any results?"

"Yeah," Fred grumbled. "We're selling my golf clubs and bowling ball."

What do you call a wife who moans and shudders and cries out during sex?

A hypocrite.

One guy sitting at the bar bragged, "When it comes to making love, you could say that my wife is the ultimate gourmet. She insists on making everything perfect."

A second guy said, "My wife's like an Italian restaurant—she gives me more and more and then some more."

A third guy grunted and said, "My wife makes love cafeteria style."

"How's that?" the other two asked.

"You have to help yourself."

What's the difference between a married man and a single guy?

A married man has a better half; a single guy gets lots of pieces.

An artist hired a very shapely model for the day. But when they arrived at his studio, they discovered that the heat had been shut off overnight and the room was freezing. The artist made some coffee while the model donned a robe. They sat around talking and sipping.

Suddenly the artist heard a car pull into the driveway outside. He looked out, then shouted to the model, "Oh my God, it's my wife. Quick, get your clothes off!"

The new recruit lined up for his first Army sick call. While he was waiting in line, the guy ahead of him turned and said, "I hear these Army docs are tough. A guy in my unit came in with corns, and they cut off his toes."

"You think that's bad," another soldier added. "Guy in my barracks had an earache, and they cut off his ear."

The new recruit screamed in panic, "I've got to get out of here? I've got herpes!"

The boss held the annual employee picnic at his house one year. He walked around the yard, introducing his wife and his eight-year-old son to the employees. Finally they came to the new young secretary. "Helen and Jamie, this is Miss Myers, who recently came to work for me."

The pretty young thing started to shake hands with the boy. But before she could, the boy took off at a run across the yard. A moment later, he returned with the garden hose.

"Jamie, what's got into you?" the boss's wife demanded of her son.

"Mom, I heard Pop say something to Mr. Schwartz the other day." He pointed to the secretary, then added. "I want to see if she really can suck a golf ball through this hose."

What happens when a guy says, "I promise I'd tell you if I had herpes?"

You discover it's a rash promise.

What's a starlet?

Someone who has to eat a long loaf to get a small role.

What's the toughest thing about acting in a porno movie?

Learning all the loins.

Why is an executive search firm like a guy in a singles bar?

They're all head hunters.

Did you hear about the porno film director who announced he wanted to find the perfect penis for his new film?

The casting director said she'd get right on it.

Why was the female stockbroker so successful?

She made sure every client got his share.

Why is hiring a high-class call girl like buying a house?

You need a very large down payment.

Did you hear about the two hookers who opened a brothel?

They referred to it as their "joint venture."

A woman decided to have a breast enlargement, so she went to see a plastic surgeon. They felt a very strong attraction for each other. After the operation, the physician moved in with her.

Unfortunately, things began to go badly. Six months later, the plastic surgeon moved out, and all the woman had left was her mammaries.

Why do so many married couples go to nudist colonies?

It's a good place to air their differences.

Why does everyone want to work at the impotency clinic?

It's a soft job.

What should a guy at an orgy say to a girl he's about to screw?

"My pace or yours?"

How do you diagnose herpes?

You start from scratch.

What do you call a guy who sells padded bras?

The fuller bust man.

Did you hear about the hooker who set up shop on the reservation?

The first night, she made a hundred bucks.

What's the definition of true happiness?

Recognizing your new secretary in a photo layout in *Playboy*.

A guy dragged himself into work one morning looking like death warmed over. A friend remarked, "Wild night, last night?"

The guy grunted. "You don't know the half of it. I got to sleep at four, and at five-thirty I was awakened by a blonde banging on my door with her shoe. The noise was so bad I couldn't go back to sleep."

"Why didn't you get up to see what she wanted?"

"I knew what she wanted. She wanted me to let her out."

A wife was suing for divorce, charging that her husband was a cleanliness fanatic. "Every single night, he insists on washing my face?"

"What's wrong with that?" the judge asked.

"Afterward, he irons it," she replied.

A drunk came staggering into the police station one night and announced, "I pushed my wife down a flight of stairs. Throw me in jail."

The desk sergeant asked, "Did you kill her?"

"I don't think so," the drunk replied. "That's why I want you to throw me in jail."

Did you hear about the wife who fooled around but wouldn't take birth control pills?

Her husband charged her with practicing license without a medicine.

One woman said to another while they were in the supermarket, "I have to buy some of those crab legs for my party Saturday night. I just love to entertain."

Her friend replied, "I used to love to entertain, too."

"What happened?"

The friend replied, "My husband started coming home."

One guy said to another guy at the bar, "You really look worried. What's the problem?"

The other guy replied, "It's marriage. I'm married to my high school sweetheart, a fantastic lover, and a terrific cook."

"So why are you worried?"

"Having three wives is illegal."

Why is reading *Playboy* like reading *National Geographic*?

In both, you see great places you'll never visit.

Heads turned when the couple walked into the room. The woman was a statuesque, stunning blonde. But most of the stares came because her husband was a short, fat, incredibly ugly man.

The couple mingled. After a few drinks, a guy came up to the husband and said, "I've just got to know. How come an ogre like you got a woman like that?"

The man replied, "When she was single, my wife had a problem. She'd never had an orgasm."

"So?"

"So I was the first guy who came along and licked it for her."

Why is the average husband like a rodeo rider?

They only stay on for 8 seconds.

A woman was sitting in the lounge at the country club, talking with a friend. She complained, "I think I'm going to have to divorce Ralph. He simply can't get it up anymore."

"You mean he's impotent?"

"Darling, how rude. I'm not talking about sex. I meant the price of my new Mercedes!"

What do you call the money you put away to hire a hooker?

Your thrust fund.

What happens when you're sailing with a beautiful girl and a storm breaks out?

You get blown ashore.

"I was in bed last night," a woman confided to her friend, "when Jack came home from the bar. He climbed in and started running his hand up and down my leg. I started to feel that old familiar sensation."

"Arousal?" the friend asked.

"Headache."

What sign did the hooker carry in the anti-nuclear rally?

"Give this piece a chance."

Why are hookers fussy?

They always have a bone to pick.

How do you know your date suffers from premature ejaculation?

He comes walking in the door.

How do you join the sex club?

It's easy—just come.

Why is sex like air?

It's no big thing, unless you aren't getting any.

Why is a hooker like a plumber?

They both do a good job of cleaning your pipes.

If a man's wife is his better half, what's his mistress?

His better hole.

Why is a woman's cunt like a roast beef sandwich?

If she shares it, you have a picnic.

What kind of secretary gets the biggest raise?

One who knows exactly what's in her boss's drawers.

What's the fastest speed at which you can make love?

68. At 69, you have to turn around and go the other way.

What's better than honor?

In her.

Why is your penis like payday?

It can't come too often.

A young farmer was having trouble with his wife. He went to see the family doctor, who advised, "You've got to be more affectionate. When you feel romantic, go up and give her a big kiss."

"But, Doc, I can't. I'm out working in the fields from dawn to dark."

The doctor thought for a moment, then said, "I've got it. Take your shotgun with you. Whenever you're in the mood for some loving, fire a blast into the air. When she hears it, she can come running."

The farmer agreed to follow the advice. The doctor didn't see him for four months. Then the farmer showed up in his office, sadder than ever.

"What's wrong?" the doctor asked. "Did you follow my advice?"

"Yup," the farmer said. "Worked great for a while. Then hunting season started a month ago, and I haven't seen her since!"

What sign did the nudist colony have over the door?

"Clothed For the Winter."

What sign was over the new brothel's front door?

"Grand Opening Sale."

Why is light beer like making love on the beach?

They're both fucking close to water.

What's the sign on the door of Planned Parenthood?

"Thank You For Not Coming."

Why was the very popular secretary nicknamed "Federal Express?"

Because she was absolutely, positively guaranteed to be there overnight.

Why are babies so fragile?

Because they're put together with one screw.

A redneck came to New York for a construction job. A few months later, he found himself called into court on a paternity suit. The girl's lawyer called the defendant to the stand and said, "Sir, could you please give me a verbatim account of your sexual encounter with my client?"

The redneck grunted. "What kind of shit are you talking? What the hell does 'verbatim' mean?"

The plaintiff's lawyer smiled condescendingly and said, "That's a technical term we lawyers use that means to give a word-by-word account of what happened. I shouldn't have expected a redneck like yourself to understand that."

The good ole boy grimaced, but he continued. "Well, we drove out by the piers. I got her in the backseat, pulled her pants off her, and started pouring the pecker to her."

"Wait a minute," the lawyer interrupted, "What does 'pouring the pecker to her' mean?"

The redneck smiled. "That's a technical term we fuckers use," he replied. "I shouldn't have expected a cocksucker like yourself to understand that."

What was the sign on the massage parlor door?

"Please come in. We knead your business."

One girl said to another, "What a bummer last night. My boyfriend forgot to bring a condom, so he made me blow him."

The other girl grimaced. "You're lucky. When my boyfriend forgets his condom, it's a pain in the ass."

A little boy walked into the bedroom one night to see his father putting it to his mother. He asked, "What are you doing?"

The father grunted, "I'm filling your mother's tank."

The little boy replied, "Well, she sure gets lousy mileage. The postman filled her just this morning."

Why is your wife like your front door?

They both have mail slots.

A woman was lying in bed late one night, unable to sleep. Finally she poked her husband awake and said, "Frank, I've got to know. If I died, would you marry again?"

"I suppose so," he replied.

"Would you sleep with her in this bed?" the wife asked.

"It's the only bed in the house," the husband replied.

"Would you make love to her?"

"Honey," the husband said, "of course. We'd be married. Now, go to sleep."

"One more question," she said. "Would you let her drive my car?"

"No," the husband replied. "She doesn't know how to drive a stick shift."

Why is your microwave like your husband?

They both heat up instantly, then go "ding" in 20 seconds.

The girl turned to her sex partner and asked, "Can you fuck me and hurt me?"

"Sure," he replied. Then he fucked her and hit her over the head with a brick.

Why are pro basketball players such lousy lovers?

They never take longer than 24 seconds to shoot.

Why is a baseball player like a loser?

His bat's in his hand four or five times a night, but he rarely scores.

Why do girls love big game hunters?

Because they go headfirst into the bush.

Anxious to impress the young starlet, the producer took her for a ride in his new Ferrari. He stomped on the accelerator, cruising up to 110 m.p.h. on the freeway. Spotting his exit, he slammed on the brakes, skidded across three lanes, sped down the exit ramp, executed a screeching turn onto a boulevard, then, for the finale, did a full 360-degree turn before coming to a stop in front of the door to his mansion.

The starlet took a moment to catch her breath. Then she turned to the producer and exclaimed, "I bet you're hard on tires."

The producer smiled. "Let's go to the bedroom. I bet it doesn't!"

The college student picked up his gorgeous coed date at her home. He'd scraped every cent together to take her to a French restaurant. To his horror, his budget was blown when she ordered three appetizers, soup, lobster, the special dessert, and a bottle of expensive champagne. When he recovered enough to talk, he asked, "What are you doing? Does your mother feed you like that at home?"

"No," she replied sweetly, "But my mother's not looking to get fucked and sucked tonight."

The well-stacked young policewoman collared the young executive on drunk driving charges. She read him his rights, reminding him, "Anything you say can and will be used against you."

Staring at her figure, he replied, "Boob, boob, boob, boob, boob . . ."

A businessman sat down next to a disconsolate friend and said, "I know you're upset about your divorce, George. But there's a lot of fish in the sea."

"I know," George replied. "The problem is, that bitch took all my bait."

What's the toughest part about being a hooker?

You can't whistle while you work.

Why are penises like designer jeans?

It takes quite a few yanks to get them off.

What would you rather be, a light bulb or a bowling ball?

It depends if you'd rather be screwed or fingered.

How do you know your marriage is in trouble?

When your wife's favorite sex aid is Pepto-Bismol.

What's the best way to attract women at a nudist colony?

Carry two glasses and twelve doughnuts.

What's a bachelor?

A man who can ball without the chain.

A gorgeous blonde was sitting at the bar, and the guy struck up a conversation. After a very cordial half hour, the guy asked, "Do you think you could love me?"

"I'm sorry," she said. "My heart belongs to another."

"The guy started to walk away. She grabbed him by the arm and added, "However, the rest of me's open to the highest bidder."

What did it say on the starlet's T-shirt?

"Made in Hollywood."

How do you know if the premiere of the new porno movie is a success?

Everyone comes.

How do you know a poet's horny?

He asks you to his apartment to check out his Longfellow.

Eyes turned when the naked woman walked into the costume party. Finally the host went up to her and said, "That's an interesting costume. What are you?"

She replied, "I'm Adam."

He said, "Pardon me, but you don't have a cock."

"Dressed like this," she answered, "I'm sure I won't have a problem finding one."

What's marriage?

A ceremony that turns your dream boat into a barge.

Why is sex like Thanksgiving?

You start out with a little thigh, a little leg, lots of breast, then move on to the stuffing.

The young starlet's marriage was on the rocks because her much older producer husband kept finding her screwing younger men. She went to her doctor and explained the problem.

The doctor replied, "I think the answer is a simple operation in which we graft a tiny portion of your ear onto your pussy."

"How will that help?" she asked.

"From now on, you'll hear your husband coming."

What do you do with 365 used rubbers?

Make them into a tire and call it a good year.

Why did God make women smell like fish?

Because cum looks like tartar sauce.

What happens if you put your panties on backward?

You get your ass chewed out.

Chapter Nine

Simply Disgusting

A man came up to a friend on the street and asked, "Who are you going to vote for in the election?"

The second man grimaced. "Why bother? All politicians are the same—they treat us all like mushrooms."

"Mushrooms?"

"Yeah," the second man replied. "They keep us in the dark and feed us nothing but shit."

What's the definition of "stress?"

The condition that results when one's mind overrides the body's basic desire to choke the living shit out of some asshole who desperately needs it.

How can you tell a guy's a real loser?

When answering machines hang up on him.

What's the cruelest thing to say to a condemned prisoner who's strapped into the electric chair?

"More power to you."

Why is a young woman like a pedophile?

They're both good at making babies.

What goes "tap-tap-tap-boom!"

A blind man in a minefield.

How can you tell a baby is ugly?

His mother finds him with a slingshot.

Why do proctologists have such extravagantly decorated offices?

They've discovered that the ends justify the means.

The girl slapped her boyfriend and demanded, "How dare you say my cunt tastes like shit?"

"Sorry," the boyfriend replied. "It was just a slip of the tongue."

Why is a necrophiliac like a taxidermist?

Whenever he finds anything dead, he mounts it.

Why did the teenage girl want to get locked up in jail?

To keep her face from breaking out.

What's a loser?

A lightning rod salesman who gets caught in a thunderstorm with samples in his hands.

A carpetlayer was installing new wall-to-wall carpeting in the family room of a home. He'd had a little too much to drink the night before, so he was in a bit of a daze as he worked. Finally he finished and stepped back to inspect the job. To his dismay, he noticed a lump right in the middle of the floor.

The thought of tearing up all the carpet churned his stomach. He patted his pockets for a moment, looking for a smoke. Then he realized his pack of cigarettes was missing. He checked his gear and his coat, but the cigarettes weren't there.

Then he had an idea. He got out a hammer, walked into the room, and began smashing the lump. It took a while, but finally the lump was so flattened that it was barely noticeable. Satisfied, he carried his tools out to his truck.

His pack of cigarettes was on the front seat. As he walked back into the house, he heard a little boy say, "Mommy, have you seen the kitten?"

Why can you trust a funeral director?

He'd be the last one to let you down.

A woman had a very severe heart attack. Her husband rushed to the hospital to find her in extremely critical condition. The doctor took him aside and said, "Your wife will be dead in a couple of hours if she doesn't get a heart transplant. Unfortunately, no suitable human donors are available. However, we've been testing a method of transplanting the heart of a cow into a human being. It's very risky, but your wife faces certain death without a transplant."

The idea of his wife having a cow's heart shocked the man, but he finally realized he had no choice. He consented to the operation. To his surprise and delight, his wife survived the operation and recovered very quickly. A month later, she went home.

Two weeks later, the doctor called the husband in and asked how his wife was making out. The man replied, "Well, I guess I'd say good and bad."

"What do you mean?"

"On the plus side," the man replied, "her grazing keeps the grass nice and short. The embarrassing thing is that she goes door to door every morning breast-feeding the neighborhood."

The guy considered himself God's gift to women. His arrogance got him in a lot of trouble. One night he tried to pick up another guy's girl in a singles bar and a fight broke out. The next thing he knew, he woke up in a hospital bed. Although he was groggy and in pain, the first thing he noticed was the big tits of a nurse leaning over him. He reached up and squeezed them hard.

The nurse screamed and jumped back. "Don't do that!" she scolded.

"Come on, baby," the guy said. "You've never had anyone like me. I know you want it."

The nurse grimaced in disgust. "No way, mack. If you're feeling horny, you'll just have to play with yourself."

The guy reached under the covers and found he was almost completely covered with bandages. "How can I do that?"

"Easy, Mr. Stud," the nurse replied. "Want to feel your organ?"

He nodded.

The nurse reached into a jar, pulled something out of formaldehyde, and said, "Here, catch."

The family had been home from vacation for three days when the little boy said, "Pop, I've been thinking about that little girl I was playing with at the shore."

"What about her?" his father replied.

"I had a lot of fun burying her in the sand. But now I'm worried."

"Why are you worried? Kids always bury each other in the sand."

"Yeah," the boy replied. "I know. But I really think I should go back and dig her up."

The obviously inebriated guest staggered up to the hostess and asked, "Do lemons have tails?"

"What?"

"Do lemons have tails?" the drunk repeated.

"Of course not," the woman replied.

"Well, then," the drunk continued. "I'm afraid I have to tell you that I've just squeezed your canary into my vodka and tonic."

What's grosser than gross?

Farting in the bathtub, then catching the bubbles with your teeth.

What's grosser than gross?

Pulling out your tampon and handing it to your kid when he wants to color.

How do you know parents hate their kid?

When they send him out for Halloween dressed as a speed bump.

How do you know parents hate their kid?

They cut his nails by sticking his hand in the blender.

How do you know parents hate their kid?

They baptize him in boiling water.

What does the Lone Ranger do in the men's room?

Take a dump, take a dump, take a dump dump dump.

What did the fly say to the spider?

"Don't eat me—I've got a wife and maggots at home!"

How do you know the teen suicide rate's getting high in your town?

The funeral home runs a back to school sale.

What's the best philosophy about teenage suicide?

"Give a kid enough rope, and he'll hang him himself."

What's teen suicide?

The best solution to the high cost of a college education.

When your teenager takes his own life, what do you get?

Unlimited use of the car on Saturday nights.

A man went to a doctor for a routine examination. When it was over, the doctor said, "You're in good shape, Mr. Reynolds, but you've got the dirtiest balls I've ever seen."

Embarrassed, the man went straight home. When he walked in the front door, he called out, "Honey, come downstairs right away. I've got something I want to talk to you about."

His wife retorted, "I can't come and talk now. I'm so busy I don't even have time to wipe my ass."

Her husband replied, "That's what I have to talk to you about."

What does it mean when an Ethiopian is "eating for two?"

Tapeworm.

How do you know your date is really ugly?

When you get a ticket for violating the leash law.

How do you know when your date is ugly and gross?

When you realize you need a pooper-scooper.

What's the definition of a loser?

A guy who plots to assassinate the vice president.

The wife had left the house that morning without a skirt she wanted to return, so she came home to get it on her lunch hour. When she walked into her bedroom, however, she nearly fainted. A ten-year-old boy was spread-eagled and naked on the bed, tied to all four bedposts. He was covered with bloody welts, evidently caused by the whip in the hand of the woman's husband. He was naked except for a black leather mask. As the woman watched in horror, her husband squatted over the boy while he pissed and shit on him.

"Harold!" the woman finally stammered. "What in heaven's name are you doing?"

"Nothing much, dear," the man replied. "I just decided to take a sick day."

What's a burp?

A fart that made a U-turn.

What's a toadstool?

What you get when you feed prunes to a toad.

What's fast talking?

Coming home from a date at 3:00 A.M. and convincing your wife your breath smells because you had tuna for dinner.

A mother walked into the bathroom to discover her son in the shower, his hand covered with cum. "How dare you do that disgusting act?" she demanded.

"Mom," he protested. "I wasn't masturbating. I was just cleaning my gun and it went off."

How do you know you're girlfriend's going to have an abortion?

You find her in the living room, knitting little body bags.

Did you hear about the new monument put up by the right-to-lifers?

The Tomb of the Unknown Fetus.

What's the preferred sex lubricant at an orgy?

3 in 1 Oil.

What's the Hell's Angels preferred sex lubricant?

20 in 1 Oil.

What's a gay's preferred sex lubricant?

Whatever's in your can.

What was the sign on the abortion clinic?

"No Fetus Can Beat Us!"

How do they end a newscast at the leper colony?

"It's 10 P.M.—do you know where your extremities are?"

Did you hear about the new "do-it-yourself" abortion?

You put a piranha in the bathwater.

How can you tell if your kid's being abused at his preschool?

His favorite activity is Blow and Smell.

What does your kid pick up at preschool?

Teacher's AIDS.

Why do ghetto kids have head lice?

So they'll always have a snack handy.

How can you tell a school is tough?

The Sex Ed. class is held in the backseat of a car.

How can you tell a girl is really fat?

Her Lacoste shirt has a little pig on the front.

How do you know necrophiliacs are selfish?

Their partners never come.

What's the remedy for child molesters?

Incesticides.

What's the outcome when a soldier has AIDS?

Dishonorable discharge.

The little boy was sitting in the kitchen when his mother entered and said, "Freddie, what are you doing here? I told you to go down to the market to get some shrimp for dinner."

"We don't need them," the boy replied.

"What do you mean, we don't need them? What am I going to put in the gumbo?"

"Sis took care of that," Freddie replied. "I heard her talking to her friend, and she said she came home with crabs last night."

What's the hardest thing about life?

Looking out for #1 while trying not to step in #2.

A cabdriver picks up a nun in lower Manhattan, and she gives him an address in Brooklyn. As they head for the tunnel, the nun confesses, "I've been a nun for 20 years, and I'm still a virgin. But I've always had a fantasy. If I could find a man who's single and who's free from sexually transmitted disease, I'd let him fuck me up the ass."

The cabdriver said, "Sister, this is your lucky day. I'm single and clean as a whistle. I'd be happy to fuck you in the ass."

The cabdriver drives to a deserted pier by the river. The sister gets out, lifts her habit, and the cabdriver rams it to her. Then they get back in the cab to finish the trip. They drive in silence for a moment, then the cabdriver says, "Sister, I have a confession to make. I'm really married."

The nun replied, "That's all right. I have a confession to make, too. My name is Bruce, and I'm on my way to a costume party."

Why should you mix prune juice with your LSD?

So you'll be a regular weirdo.

What's the heaviest thing in the world?

A piss. Even Superman can't hold it.

What's the sharpest thing in the world?

A fart. It can go through any fabric without making a hole.

Why are women like dogshit?

The older they get, the easier they are to pick up.

What's the difference between spinach and boogers?

Not everyone likes the taste of spinach.

What's the best thing to do if there are flies at your picnic?

Take a shit a few feet away to keep them busy.

What's bad taste?

Making obscene phone calls to an AIDS telethon.

Where does the golden shower freak look for telephone numbers?

In the yellow pages.

How can you tell a really tough school?

In biology class, they dissect a frogman.

What happens when you ask for a golden shower but the hooker starts to shit on you?

Tell her she's got the wrong number.

What's a two-dollar abortion?

Douche with Drâno.